Wine 123

All you need to know about wine in 90 minutes or less.

Monika Elling

FOREWORD

Dear Wine Lover,

Whether you are a newly-minted enthusiast, an experienced collector, or someone in between, I would bet that at some point in your life you have pondered one, or more, of the following questions when trying to select that perfect bottle.

> "What do I need to know to make the 'right' selection for tonight's meal? my collection? to gift?"
>
> "How much do I need to spend to get a good bottle of wine, really?"
>
> "Why am I being asked what kind of wine do I like when all want is something 'good'?"
>
> "What am I supposed to say about this wine to my family, friends, and even to my business colleagues?"
>
> "How can I look and sound confident about wine choices without simply quoting some critic's review?"

With so much wine out there and so much information available, it's easy to feel overwhelmed with the thought of picking a good bottle.

There will forever be more and more wine available to us from all corners of the globe. With wine producing regions that spread far and wide, winemaking is an ancient, yet still rapidly growing industry. From Greece to Mexico, India to Uruguay, new wine regions are popping up everywhere. We are experiencing an explosion of wine brands, popular styles and grape varieties. The good news is that today we have more choices than ever before of high-quality wines from all over the world.

Odds are you'll need to rely on some expertise to help you make the best possible decision. My goal is to give you a compass through this crazy maze of choices, while guiding you to an enjoyable and relaxed wine experience. It is not about having or learning all the answers, but to be in a position to ask the right questions. Focus on what you enjoy now, so you can know what to enjoy in the future.

If the above situation resonates, this book is for you. I want to free you from the grasp of the "expert" and empower you to trust your palate. This is not meant to be a lecture, nor is this meant to be a wine bible. Consider this your cheat-sheet from an industry insider, so let's have some fun!

Is this everything there is to know about wine? Not by a mile. However, the information inside these pages will be enough for you to look and sound, comfortable and confident as you are either walking the aisles at your local shop, or thumbing your way through an award-winning restaurant wine list.

Test cases for this book are my family and friends who call, text, or email me from restaurants and wine shops about which wine to choose for the occasion. I would like to teach all of them to think and drink independently, make some good decisions, and discover for themselves the magic and thrill of a great bottle of wine.

CHEERS!

The Author

CHAPTER 1- WOW: BASIC PRINCIPLES

CHAPTER 2- BURGUNDY: A SNAPSHOT

CHAPTER 3- BORDEAUX: THE ORIGINAL RED BLEND

CHAPTER 4- PINOT NOIR: THE REALITIES

CHAPTER 5- OLD WORLD VS NEW WORLD

CHAPTER 6- THE SCARY RESTAURANT WINE LIST

CHAPTER 7- SCREW IT

CHAPTER 8- BUBBLY

CHAPTER 9- DESSERT IN A GLASS

CHAPTER 10- PINK IS IN

CHAPTER 11- HOW TO LOOK GOOD DRINKING WINE

CHAPTER 1. WOW: BASIC PRINCIPLES

Grüner Veltliner from Austria, Vernaccia from Italy, Syrah from California, Torrontes from Argentina. It is enough to have your head spin! Consider the sheer volume of wine entering the global marketplace and flooding retail shelves. Realistically, no one can keep up with the amount of information available. In all likelihood, the strange grape names, or varieties, leave you befuddled and ready to make a mad dash for the nearest big name Cabernet Sauvignon or Chardonnay stacked at the end of the aisle.

This doesn't have to be your fate. How can you navigate so many interesting new brands, varieties and exciting packages?

In order to move beyond this state of confusion, I want to show you a simple way to evaluate wine regardless of country of origin or grape variety.

No matter which type of wine you enjoy drinking on a regular basis, the simplest way to think about wine is by weight, or rather, mouthfeel. Light, medium and heavy are basic descriptions, and those terms apply to what I call the **Weight of Wine (WOW) Scale**, for both red and white wines.

The quickest way to recognize **WOW** is by color. Consider pale straw-colored yellow as a light white **(1)**, while a somewhat darker yellow color is medium **(2)**, and a rich, golden-color as heavy in the mouth (or "on the palate") **(3)**.

For red wine, a somewhat translucent red is considered light **(1)**, while a richer and deeper ruby color is medium **(2)**, and a dark, nearly black, inky color is a heavy weight red wine **(3)**.

Weight of Wine Index (WOW) ©

1　　　　2　　　　3

The **WOW** will open up a world of natural experimentation and many choices, in recognizing your preferences. For example, if you believe the light colored Pinot Noir **(1)** to be your favorite choice in red wines, we can make the assumption that you will favor many other light bodied reds. This allows for an intelligent selection moving from something familiar (Pinot Noir), to another type of grape or blend (like Barbera).

Next we need to address the issue of wine in oak, or rather, the degree to which oaky flavors are tasted in wine. When producers prepare to make a wine, one thing they will decide upon is how much, if any, of the wine in question will be touched by oak. For the most part, wines are aged in either stainless steel containers or oak barrels. Occasionally, the same wine is aged in both, then blended by the winemaker before bottling. You probably already associate oak barrels with wine production, but keep in mind that many wines, especially light, aromatic white wines, are never aged in oak barrels. Those types of white wines, as is the case with many light & fruity red wines, are only aged in stainless steel containers.

And why is this important? It is essential to understand that the length of time a wine is placed in oak barrels has a direct impact on the price, flavor and **WOW**. When you are tasting a dark red, jammy Cabernet Sauvignon that feels like a meal in your mouth, or an intense, buttery Chardonnay, your palate should be telling you that the rich mouth-feel is not only based on the type of grape(s) the winemaker used, but also the length of time that the wine was aged in oak barrels. Some of the most commonly used descriptors about oaky flavors include terms such as, 'buttery' and 'vanilla' in describing the aromas and flavors. Great winemakers strive for balance between the flavors of meticulously farmed fruit and that of fine oak barrels. Conversely, many bulk winemakers use oak chips rather than barrels to mask the end product's less-than-perfect fruit. The better the fruit, the more important it is to make a wine that allows the fruit to shine on its own, in a balanced way, and not be overwhelmed by oak flavors. Judicious use of oak depends on the potential of the wine and stylistic direction of the winemaker. The amount and type of oak barrels used also has a direct impact on price. When a top French barrel costs $1,300 dollars, it is easy to see how oak usage can drive up the price of wine.

Secondly, alcohol levels tend to also influence **WOW**. Higher alcohol adds a broader mouthfeel and added viscosity, leading to a heavier **WOW**. As you swirl a glass of wine, you will see the legs or tears on the side of the glass. This is more pronounced as the alcohol levels increase with certain wines.

Domestic Merlot generally tends to be a mid-weight red **(2)**, flexible with many types of dishes. Merlot drinkers may find a natural progression to Malbec from Argentina or France, which would deliver a similar **WOW** factor.

If you are a domestic Cabernet Sauvignon **(3)** drinker, odds are that you would actually enjoy many other types of full-bodied red wines such as Australian Shiraz or Super Tuscans. Next time you are making a selection, try to embrace the transition by choosing other bold red blends which may have Cabernet Sauvignon as the main blending variety, including wines from Bordeaux and California . Similar style wine like Amarone and Super Tuscans will satisfy your palate, which is seeking a heavy-hitting red.

The same scenario applies to white wines. Those who enjoy light bodied Pinot Grigio **(1)** will gravitate to varieties, such as Verdejo from Spain or Falanghina from Italy.

A Sauvignon Blanc would be looking at a more flavorful, medium weight wine **(2)**, which opens up a whole new world of options. One can consider an Italian Vernaccia, Friulano or Arneis, not to mention a dry white Bordeaux (Bordeaux Blanc), which is typically a Sauvignon Blanc/Semillion blend.

It should be no surprise that California Chardonnay is considered a heavy weight wine **(3)**, mostly due to the warm climate and liberal use of oak. These wines tend to be aged 6-12 months, or more, in oak. If this is something you enjoy, it is high time to venture to another warm region, such as Australia.

As a simple guide, start assigning a **(1)**, **(2)** or **(3)** from the **WOW** scale to every wine you come across; make this a regular mental exercise. Racy, aromatic, fruity white wines without oak fall in the lightest category **(1)**, while richer, lightly oaked or blended whites are a **(2)**, and heavily oaked whites or whites with higher percentages of alcohol are a **(3)**. Light colored, fruit forward, easy mouth-feel reds are a category **(1)**, while medium bodied reds with a touch of oak are a **(2)**, and dark colored, heavy reds, generally aged in new oak with higher alcohol are a **(3)**. With just a little practice you will get the hang of this, and at the same time, odds are good your selections will be geared towards particular **WOW** group.

Grape Variety	Color	Flavor Guide	WOW
Dry to semi-dry Riesling	Pale Straw	Tart apple, white peach, slate	1
Pinot Grigio/ Pinot Gris	Pale Yellow	Fruity, fresh, crisp	1
Chardonnay (Unoaked)	Light gold	Apple, minerality, citrus	1
Sauvignon Blanc	Pale Straw	Citrus, crisp, racy	2
Chardonnay (oaked)	Golden	Apple, Tropical Fruit, Buttery	3
Pinot Noir	Light Red	Berry, earth, cinnamon	1
Merlot	Medium Red	Red and black fruit, cocoa powder	2
Syrah/Shiraz	Medium Red to purple	Cherries, raspberry, plumb	2
Cabernet Sauvignon	Dark Red	Black current, black cherry, licorice, vanilla	3
Tokaj Aszu	Deep Gold	Honey, apricot, tropical fruit	3

Is this a perfect guideline? No, however, this will help to take some of the guesswork out of selecting your preferred style of wine both at the store and at the restaurant. You can confidently ask your retailer or sommelier regarding the **WOW** factor when considering a **(1)**, **(2)** or **(3)** weight scale. With an understanding of the **WOW** scale, you will quickly develop your own sense of how to evaluate a wine, and this will assist you make magic with food and wine pairing.

One quick rule of thumb is the concept of a light, medium or heavy protein dish, paired with a wine of similar weight. From chicken to steak, the color and preparation of the meat can be a quick and easy guideline, e.g., light colored meat with light wine, and so forth. Ultimately you are striving to balance complementary flavors that when married, add immeasurably to the tasting experience.

There is now a trend to serve red wine with fish. If you think of fish as delicate and lightly flavored, it is completely acceptable to pair it with light, elegant red wine, specifically something from category **(1)**. Fish prepared with tomatoes, roasted vegetables and heavier spices creates a more robust dish. You can certainly stay with a category **(1)** wine, but this is your chance to to move up the weight scale, in both red and white. The overall impact of the dish - **(1, 2** or **3)** by strength of flavor - can dictate the weight of the chosen wine.

When pairing with spicy foods such as Asian and Indian cuisine, it is best to stick with aromatic white wines **(1)** such as dry to off-dry Riesling. The wine's brisk acidity and fresh fruity flavors will balance the heat and spice of the dish to deliver a mouth-watering experience.

Simply put, think of food and wine pairing as 2+2=5. If the impact of the food and wine together results in a better tasting wine and a more flavorful dish, that is a great pairing. If you wind up with a 2+2=1 experience, then the pairing missed the mark. It is not the end of the world! Trust your taste buds to tell you whether the combination made the meal a more enjoyable experience, or not. After all, that is what matters the most.

SUMMARY:

- Reduce wine confusion by concentrating on **WOW**.
- When pondering mouthfeel, mentally assign **(1)** to lightly weighted wines, **(2)** to medium weighted, and **(3)** to heavy weighted.
- Weight of Wine is dictated by a combination of things, including the type of grape variety, ripeness, the winemaker's oak-treatment and percentage of alcohol in the wine.
- Light wines will have less oak treatment, may be drier, and probably have lower alcohol.
- Light, medium or full-bodied are descriptions to categorize the weight of white. (**WOW**)
- Light-colored meats and lightly prepared dishes pair best with light wines, both whites and reds. Same principle applies to medium and heavy meats/dishes and appropriately weighted wines.
- Light colored meat/fish preparation typically pairs better with light wines **(1)**, and progressively darker colored meats require darker, heavier wines **(3)**.
- Fuller bodied wines tend to have more alcohol and are aged in oak barrels.
- Always consider the sauce, spices and level of heat. For example, spicy Asian dishes are best served with racy, aromatic white wines or slightly sweet and low in alcohol wines in the **(1)** category.
- The use of oak barrels can add significantly to the price of wine.
- Ask your sommelier or favorite retailer for a different type of wine in the **WOW** category that you normally enjoy, and expand your palate.
- There are no correct or incorrect answers. Let your taste buds decide!

CHAPTER 2. BURGUNDY: A SNAPSHOT

A surprising number of people, even wine novices, are familiar with the term Burgundy. It never ceases to amaze me when people who claim to love Chardonnay, don't order white Burgundy. Similarly, there are those who are partial to Pinot Noir, but may never consider red Burgundy for dinner.

Let's clarify what this all means and take a look at this legendary French wine region. There are two core grapes grown in Burgundy; one red and one white. The red is Pinot Noir, while the white is Chardonnay. This is essential information if you enjoy those grapes. A Pinot Noir fan can start selecting wines from red Burgundy producers, while a Chardonnay aficionado should readily expand to sipping white Burgundy. From a **WOW** standpoint, Pinot Noir is most often considered a light-bodied **(1)** red wine, unless it comes from a producer in a warmer region. Add oak treatment and ever-greater fruit intensity and you'll have a Pinot Noir that sits squarely in the category **(2)** on the **WOW** scale.

Chardonnay is a more complex **WOW** question, since California producers tend to produce their wines with heavier oak treatment and higher alcohol levels than winemakers from Burgundy. Generally, heavily-oaked Chardonnay falls into the full-bodied **(3)** category, while moderately oaked Chardonnay falls to be medium-bodied **(2)**. Low-moderate oak treatment is more typical of entry-level French 'old world' styles.

In addition to the name of the winery, the multiple French words on Burgundy bottles refer to the particular vineyard and appellation (place of origin), of which there are many within the designated Burgundy wine-growing region. The leading vineyards offer a "Grand Cru" designation, signifying the "best-of-the-best" vineyard sites within a specific village. Lower down the quality ladder is "Premier Cru", followed by the "Village" wines and finally he Regionally designated wines, e.g., Bourgogne Rouge. Keep in mind that these designations only speak to the potential of the vineyard and the wines. There are significant differences of quality between the producers themselves, which explains price variations.

The French have historically not placed the words Pinot Noir or Chardonnay on the label of a Burgundy wine, although this is changing, especially on the labels of entry level, inexpensive Burgundy. Instead, they tell you the name of the village and appellation so you can determine whether you like the influence of terroir in the wine. Terroir is the French term for the land and environment in which the grapes grow, and this is an essential factor for wine professionals in determining baseline characteristics of wine from a given producer, as well as an appellation. This is why some wines are so highly prized by those who understand the overall context. Burgundy collectors go crazy for certain producers and vineyards, as they believe the grapes grown in a given area best reflect the terroir.

Wines from the Chablis region tend to be minimally touched by oak, if at all; gorgeous, yet austere with a flinty, mineral quality to them. The Puligny or Chassagne Montrachet region wines are wonderfully complex, balancing fruit, oak and minerality. It would be difficult to confuse an inexpensive, entry-level white Burgundy (2) with an oaky California Chardonnay (3), simply because most Burgundy producers at this level utilize a restrained level of French oak. This is combined with the regions' unique minerality, which allows for very distinctive flavors.

On the flip side, Pinot Noir in Burgundy has a tendency for sublime elegance, which may appear to be lighter than a typical California Pinot Noir. Think of entry-level red Burgundy as light, elegant red wines, which will taste soft, but complex, on the palate. A nuance of layered flavors is a typical descriptor for Burgundian Pinot Noir.

As any serious wine professional will tell you, the words "cheap" and Pinot Noir do not fall into the same sentence. Growing Pinot Noir is a huge challenge anywhere, as it is a fickle grape that needs to be tended and cajoled, therefore labor extensive. This level of care is an expensive proposition, therefore pricing for good quality Pinot Noir will easily be above $20. Burgundy wine prices for both red and white wines are even higher, and these wines are probably best reserved for special occasions. The price also reflects great demand, as the Burgundy region has long established credentials on the collectable fine wine circuit. Still, if you enjoy Chardonnay or Pinot Noir, this is an experience not to be missed.

A less expensive proposition would be a Gamay wine from the region, such as Beaujolais. Gamay wines are light to medium bodied on the palate, displaying a round, easily drinkable style, and mostly meant to be drunk young. They see little if any oak treatment, tend to have lower alcohol, and are not meant for aging. As a result, Gamay is a solid and cost effective alternative to Pinot Noir.

For the most part, Cabernet Sauvignon lovers are not fans of Pinot Noir or Gamay, and essentially stay away from these varieties. An elegant and light **WOW** is at odds with bold and full-mouthfeel wines. This is not to say the lines aren't crossed, rather, it's more about typical preferences that speak to individual taste.

SUMMARY:
- Terroir is the French term for the land and environment in which the grapes grow
- Burgundy labels do not typically indicate the type of grape inside the bottle, rather the name of the Village and broader appellation from which the wine comes.
- Burgundy features two core grapes, one white, Chardonnay and one red, Pinot Noir
- In the South of Burgundy there is a region, Beaujolais where they grow Gramay
- Chablis is a white wine made from the Chardonnay grape, and is also a Burgundy appellation even though is geographically situated separately and further north of any other wine region in Burgundy.
- Chablis is usually an un-oaked, medium-bodied white made of Chardonnay, typically with a **(1) WOW** factor.
- Grand Cru Vineyards signify the best of the best, followed by Premier Cru, Village and finally regional designations.

CHAPTER 3. BORDEAUX: THE ORIGINAL RED BLEND

Moving onto a very simplified version of the legendary Bordeaux wines of France, keep in mind the six red varieties that make up Bordeaux wines are principally Cabernet Sauvignon, Merlot and Cabernet Franc, blended to different degrees with Malbec, Petit Verdot and Carmenere. Red Bordeaux wines are blends of these varieties, and winemakers determine the exact proportion of the various grapes based on where in Bordeaux they are planted, as well as each year's vintage conditions. Bordeaux producers are identified by the name of their 'chateau' with wines that have a consistent style from one vintage year to the next. Quality of the grapes, however, can vary from one vintage to the next, which can produce wines that are overtly fruity or earthy, full flavored and plush or more elegant and reserved. The art of blending was first popularized in Bordeaux, hence, our reference to The Original Red Blend.

The Gironde River and the tributaries that feed it geographically split Bordeaux. For simplicity's sake we can divide vineyard-growing regions into Left Bank and Right Bank. Wines from the Left Bank appellations are dominated by the Cabernet Sauvignon grape, while Right Bank wines are predominantly Merlot-based.

How do you know which Bordeaux wine is Left and which is Right Bank? If the label says "St. Emilion" or "Pomerol", it is from the Right Bank. All of the rest are from the Left Bank.

In 1855 Bordeaux wines on the Left Bank were classified into five categories as determined by price: First Growth, Second Growth, Third Growth, Fourth Growth and Fifth Growth. The top Bordeaux First Growth wines are unaffordable for most people these days. This is especially so from a great vintage year. However, regardless of status, many of the leading Chateaux offer wines from second labels that can deliver extraordinary wines at a somewhat more reasonable price point. The flagship wines of the top Chateau labeled "Grand Cru Classe en 1855", with other releases from those wineries are typically considered second labels. The second label is made from grapes that either did not make it into the flagship wine, or were sourced from younger vines on the estate, which is reflected in the lower price.

The best grapes picked during harvest from the best vineyards go into the Grand Cru Classe wines, while lesser grapes go into the second and third labels. Second and third label wines are better values as they use fruit that did not make it into the flagship, and typically those wines are aged for less time in 2 or 3-year-old oak barrels. All of those decisions drive the price down compared to the flagship label. Grand Cru wines are aged for years in new oak barrels. The cost of the oak barrels and inventory, increases pricing as the wines are later released to market.

If you are looking for Bordeaux to drink tonight, you have two choices. Consider that Cabernet Sauvignon will need time to age, so if money is not an issue, buy an older vintage of a Left Bank Chateau. Start with a wine from 15 years ago and go backwards in time, as your budget allows. Expect to pay several hundred or even thousands of dollars per bottle for Left Bank Bordeaux Grand Cru Classe wines.

With few exceptions, the more budget conscious choice is to get wines from St. Emilion or Pomerol as they will taste better, much sooner than the Left Bank wines. This is mainly because Merlot is the base wine, and Merlot is an early ripening, softer grape than Cabernet Sauvignon. It will be more round and fruity on the palate, and simply more accessible even from a pricing perspective. Look for St. Emilion Grand Cru, and ask for the second or third label from the Estate to have a great value wine. Price range is from $20 -$200+ per bottle. Generally speaking, St. Emilion Bordeaux wines in the $50-$75 range are terrific.

White Bordeaux wine is made from a blend of Sauvignon Blanc and Semillon, in varying proportions. Dry, white Bordeaux is light, elegant, and a terrific food match due to the acidity of Sauvignon Blanc. It is also very reasonably priced. Sauternes is the Bordeaux appellation where they make dessert wines, primarily from Semillon. Those wines have high sugar content and are generally very expensive, therefore tend to be an occasional treat for most wine lovers.

SUMMARY:
- Bordeaux is divided into Right and Left Bank, and has three dominant red varieties, Cabernet Sauvignon, Merlot and Cabernet Franc
- Bordeaux labels do not list the varieties, so you won't find Cabernet or Merlot on the label. Rather they feature the name of the Chateau and the appellation/wine district.
- Bordeaux producers are identified by the name of their 'chateau' with wines that have a consistent style from one vintage year to the next. Quality of the grapes, however, can vary from one vintage to the next, which will produce wines that are overtly fruity or earthy, full flavored and plush or more elegant and reserved.
- Left Bank Bordeaux wines are Cabernet Sauvignon based with Cabernet Franc and Merlot blended in. The wines are robust and complex, with aging capability.
- Left Bank Grand Cru wines are collectively the most expensive wines in the world.
- Grand Cru Classe signifies the top-label wine of a leading Chateau. Right Bank wines consist of predominantly Merlot, with touches of Cabernet Sauvignon and Cabernet Franc. They tend to be ready-to-drink earlier then Left Bank wines due to the suppleness of Merlot.
- Right Bank St. Emilion wines are the best values, in Bordeaux ranging from $25 -$150 per bottle.
- St. Emilion and Pomerol are Right Bank wines. The rest are Left Bank.
- White Bordeux is a blend of Sauvignon Blanc and Semillon.
- Sauternes Dessert Wines are also made from these two white grapes.
- Sauternes dessert wines are some of the most expensive wines in the world

CHAPTER 4. PINOT NOIR: THE REALITIES

Can anything be more boring than drinking what everyone else is drinking? Let's take the Pinot Noir craze. This is a fad started by a movie called Sideways, which disses Merlot, extols Pinot Noir, and there you have it. It is time to turn that type of thinking upside down. All the while keep in mind; I do actually enjoy a good Pinot Noir.

Today, many people are buying a $10-$15 bottle of wine called Pinot Noir. They say they "LOVE" the wine and believe they are experiencing the grape as it is meant to be. The bad news is this is completely false. Good Pinot Noir under $20 is hard to find, and at $30 we begin to taste things that resemble what the grape is meant to show. Therefore, good Pinot Noir for me is still more of a special occasion wine. You are far more likely to find more under $15 day-to-day options with other red varieties simply due to the relatively higher premium placed on Pinot Noir. Good, or great, Pinot Noir can be exceptional - and very expensive. It is a difficult, fickle grape to grow, and creates a tremendous challenge and yes, opportunity for winemakers around the world. The most famous and historic home to Pinot Noir is Burgundy, France, but excellent examples of the grape are grown in Oregon, New Zealand, California, and a few other places. The grape needs a rather cool climate to grow well and show its potential. Its characteristics are hints of earth, berry flavors, strawberries and minerality. The grape at its best, offers layers and layers of complexity and elegance. At an entry level price, main characteristics of some of the better tasting Pinot Noir are clean, bright red fruit, round soft tannins and a short, but pleasant finish. The worst examples offer thin, weak aromas and flavors, with a bitter finish.

More than most other grapes, Pinot Noir reflects the environment from which it comes. In a nutshell, Pinot Noir is expensive because it is tough to make. As we discussed in the Burgundy Chapter, red Burgundies are categorically the very highest priced Pinot Noir. In California, prices have sky rocketed and a new generation of premium Oregon Pinot Noirs are priced up there as well. You can find some reasonable values from New Zealand, but there, too, is an upward pricing trend. Since Pinot Noir is in high demand at $15 and under in America, many large wineries are blending domestic Pinot Noir with other grapes such as Syrah to produce better results and more quantity. It is also worthwhile considering other Pinot Noir producing countries such as Germany, France, Chile, as prices can be more reasonable.

Consider the alternatives. If you are in the mood for a light bodied red wine **(1)** to go with dinner, it is sometimes better to go with a "Best of Category" wine than to drink a bottle of a premium grape. I recommend that you consider a Grenache from Spain, France, Australia or New Zealand, a Zweigelt from Austria, Montepulciano D'Abruzzo or Dolcetto from Italy; perhaps snap up a Cotes Du Rhône or Beaujolais from France. All light, fruity reds at excellent quality levels to be had under $20.

While Merlot has had a challenging run in the last decade, very nice wines can be had from this grape at reasonable prices. Don't be shy about seeking out options. As American Pinot Noir prices have moved up rapidly due to increased demand, there are very few values left. That creates an opportunity for well-priced domestic Merlot, and you should take advantage of this by exploring the grape in the $20 and under category.

In Chapter two we learned that in Bordeaux's St. Emilion region, the primary grape is Merlot. Merlot is the most important widely produced variety in the Bordeaux region. It ripens early, and is reliable for providing solid sugar levels at harvest. It isn't fickle, and weathers most climactic issues well. Therefore, Merlot can deliver a good value in the $20 and under category, and can produce spectacular wines. Keep in mind, legendary "Petrus" is one of the most expensive wines in the world, and is made 100% from Merlot grapes.

SUMMARY:
- Good quality Pinot Noir will often run you $25 and up - be prepared!
- If you are looking for a light, elegant, flexible red wine for significantly less, look at Grenache from Spain, France or Australia; Zweigelt from Austria; Montepulciano D'Abruzzo or Dolcetto from Italy; Cotes Du Rhône or Beaujolais from France. All can be had under $20.
- Be prepared to pay upwards of $20 for domestic Pinot Noir, and often you will find more reasonable options from other producing nations such as Germany, New Zealand, France and Chile.
- Be very open to Merlot and Merlot blends, as the grape is a core ingredient of many red wine blends.
- Merlot is a deeper color than Pinot Noir, with also more robust, rounder mouthfeel. **WOW (2+)**.
- You can find reasonably priced, delicious Merlot from California and France at $20 and under. When looking at France, keep in mind St. Emilion wines are predominantly Merlot base.
- One of the most famous and expensive wines in the world is Petrus, which is made from 100% Merlot with a **WOW** of **(3)**.
- Be open to ALL varieties, as there is a whole world of flavor to explore.

CHAPTER 5. OLD WORLD VS. NEW WORLD: ENTER THE WINE SNOB

Stylistically and geographically, wine is often said to fall into two broad categories: Old World and New World. Old World is classified as the core European producing regions. New World includes North and South American, Australia, New Zealand and South Africa, even though these locations have had wine for hundreds of years.

There are good, bad, and great wines from both worlds, and of course, a host of differences based on individual producers. The wine snob enters the equation when you hear the words "I only drink Bordeaux" or "I don't care for New World Wines". A true wine professional or even a knowledgeable wine lover will never make such a statement. The sign of a wine pro is that they enjoy a variety of wines from every corner of the world and continue to experiment with wines from a wide variety of established and new producers. That is not to say one can't have a preference, but an open mind and palate are the most important tools for a wine lover.

Old World wine characteristics play to tradition, as history of those wine regions have been established for many hundreds of years. In winemaking styles, the overall direction has been to create wines with a great deal of structure, which need time in the bottle to evolve. The grapes are picked at lower sugar levels than typical for the New World wines and alcohol levels tend to be lower as well. The aromatics (the nose) on Old World wines tend to be more muted, and the wines need aeration or decanting well in advance of consumption. They are often "tight" and evolve upon opening as oxygen enters the scene. That is the importance of the "swirl", as it releases a wine's full aromatics and flavor.

With time, most Old World wine becomes approachable, providing layers and layers of nuanced, magnificent flavor. This process can take years, sometimes decades, depending on the region and style of the wine.

In the exploration of a wine list, one can see wines from 15 or 20 years ago and the sticker price will be high. Such pricing is due to the fact that the producer and restaurateur will have had to age the wine, keeping it inventory for years, adding to the cost of purchase.

All this aside, there is no guarantee that you will actually enjoy the wine! If your palate and sensibilities favor more fruit driven, approachable wines, you might struggle with the complexities of an old Burgundy or Bordeaux, and find many Italian Barolos tight and lean. It is absolutely normal to have those impressions and it does not make you a wine weakling. There is power in the knowledge that you can prefer whatever wine you like!

Now that you are armed with this information, you will be amused to find how often you will come across these ideas, mostly from consumers. Listen to your friends, family and business associates and gauge their wine-speak. Remember, true wine professionals are open to everything and always look to explore something new, even if they have some special preferences.

New World really begins with Californian wines as they set a standard for high quality wines in the modern era. Getting past the Prohibition Era and jug wines of Ernest and Julio Gallo, some remarkable developments in both viticulture and winemaking since the 1960's have paved the way for the outstanding wines of today. Winemaking in California has been evolutionary and filled with a rich history of Europeans sharing their winemaking culture and skills since settling in California in the 1800's.

The veritable father of the Californian wine industry is Count Agoston Haraszty, a Hungarian noble man who is credited with importing over 600 cuttings of rootstock from throughout Europe and planting them in Sonoma, California. His winemaking endeavor was Buena Vista winery, which is still thriving today.

With other leading personalities such as the Mondavis, California winemaking over the last five decades set the tone for other New World regions, within and, beyond the United States. Quality has grown tremendously, so much so that in the renowned "Tasting of Paris" in May of 1976, a panel of world-class critics chose Chateau Montelena Chardonnay as the winner, over a renowned selection of Burgundy wines, as the top performer in a blind tasting. This set the wine world on fire, and as California established quality standards, other New World producers followed.

Today's New World styles are viewed as fruit driven, immediately approachable, with higher phenolic ripeness and alcohol levels that can come across as perceived sweetness. When referencing the full fruit flavors and modern, polished smoothness in New World wines, critics are often talking about these characteristic. The wines may have a bit higher alcohol content, as sugar levels at harvest drive this component during the fermentation process. Nevertheless, quality of a wine is dictated by balance, which refers to the wine's concentration of fruit, brightness of acid, alcohol, and other structural components that combine to create an overall sensory experience.

Without question, the structure and beauty of Old World wines are greatly enhanced with their marriage with food. European consumption has always been about wine as an essential addition to any meal. Wines from the different regions of Europe have been refined over centuries to best reflect and complement the cuisine of their respective region from which they are produced. Once enjoyed with food, Old World wines present in harmony with all flavors of the dishes. Conversely, New World wines can be enjoyed well with meals, but also on their own, as the round and softer tannins do not require food for balance.

Stylistically you do not need to favor one over the other. You can easily choose to enjoy great Chianti with your lasagna, while the next day select a Napa Valley Chardonnay with your grilled chicken.

New World wine can be more difficult to match with food, since the ripeness, alcohol levels and intensity can overshadow flavors. Drinking Old World wines without food can be a challenge, since many of the wines will make your mouth pucker and get you salivating for food to balance. Here are some descriptors you can easily remember:

Old World Style	New World Style
Elegant, Finesse	Opulent, Rich
Lean	Lush, Dense
Restrained	Fruit Forward
Needs Food	Excellent on its own

SUMMARY:
- Stylistically wine can fall into two categories; Old World and New World
- Old World refers to European and European-styled wine making regions.
- Structure, finesse and tight tannins that open up and evolve over time characterize Old World wines.
- Old World wines express better with food, while New World wines are often drinkable without a food component.
- New World includes North and South America, Australia, New Zealand, South Africa.
- New World wines are approachable, "ready-to-drink" upon opening, and typically have a round mouth-feel.
- New World wines harvest at higher sugar levels and ripeness, which allows for rounder, smoother tannins, but also higher levels of alcohol.
- Many American wine lovers will find Old World tight, lean and lacking fruit. It is ok to prefer New World wines on one occasion, while selecting Old World wines at other times.
- True wine professionals (and anyone with wine confidence) may have preferences, but fulfillment in wine tasting is to enjoy and explore wines from all regions.
- Best wines are all about balance, as that is what great winemaking is all about.

CHAPTER 6. THE SCARY RESTAURANT WINE LIST

Tonight you are at a restaurant, with new business associates in town, looking to land a deal over good conversation and hopefully a nice bottle or two of wine. As the owner of a small business, your budget isn't exactly unlimited. The sommelier appears with something that resembles a phone book and you begin to peruse the various sections on Bordeaux, California, Germany and more. Quickly you begin to feel your confidence wane. "Where do I begin?" you ask yourself.

Sensing your dilemma, the Sommelier leans over you as you are furtively glancing at the wine list. Their recommendation follows and you succumb, without really understanding why you were just talked into a wine that was three times the budget you had in mind. Here is how to take better control of the situation.

For dinners that matter, I urge you to download the wine list in advance, or stop by the restaurant for a preview. That preparation pays off in spades, and allows for the most appropriate choice at the target budget.

The best sommeliers in the business are extraordinarily good at their jobs, so consider them your allies. After all, it is their job to know and understand all the wines on their list and also their responsibility to keep up-to-date on the restaurant's changing menu. My goal is to give you a few simple rules to follow that will better enlist their assistance. Consider the dining experience as an opportunity to try wines not tasted before, and a chance to experiment. All the while, you want to feel comfortable that your wine picks will meet and exceed expectations. These tips will help you to be perceived as knowledgeable and wine savvy in front of your audience.

In a typical dining scenario, it is important to take early control of the situation. You sit with your companions and are handed the menu and the wine list. If the Sommelier approaches and asks what wine you would like to order, tell him to come back when you have had a chance to review the meal selections. This will signal that you understand food and wine pairing. We have discussed Weight of Wine (**WOW**) in Chapter 1 and that will be your most important guide. For light style in food selection, safe bets are light white or red wines **WOW (1)**, while hearty, rich dishes can handle a bold, structured wine choice **WOW (3)**. When one bottle is meant to cover a variety of meal choices at the table, strive for a red or white that is a **WOW (2)**.

To estimate quantities, you can expect to get 4-5 glasses of wine per bottle. If there are only two of you with similar style of food selections, it is then a simple choice in terms of **WOW**. When you order steak and your colleague orders fish, you can always go for wines by the glass and that way you can both have exactly what you want. However, if the fish dish is a hearty one such as Cioppino, which is seafood in a spicy tomato sauce served over linguini, then you can easily choose a full-bodied wine **WOW (3)** that will also be perfect for your partner's steak. Keep the Weight of Wine (**WOW**) always in mind. Once you made your food choices and have settled on the idea of ordering a white or a red, or both, for the table, ask the Sommelier the following type questions, and do include a price range:

"I am looking for a medium bodied red wine in the $75-$85 per bottle price range as well as a light bodied, fruity white in the $45-$55 range. What have you tasted this week that you enjoyed and would like to recommend?"

Or

"I enjoy Bordeaux and see that you have a very nice selection. Mostly I prefer a Merlot based Bordeaux and I am looking to spend no more than $100. What vintage is drinking well right now, and which wine can you recommend?

Or

"I would like a Pinot Noir and see that you have an extensive selection from all over the world. Generally, my preference is Oregon Pinot Noir, but I tend to drink (name the ones you have tried) and would like to try something new in the $125-150 (or whatever price point) category. What have you tried lately that you could recommend?

Or

"What have you tasted this week that struck you as an exciting, full bodied red wine in the $75-$125 category?"

Do not be concerned about losing face by naming your price range. A Sommelier will point to a best of category wine within the range you provide. Sommeliers feel at ease when a patron provides that information, as it clarifies for them how they need to approach a selection.

The best restaurants are those whose wine directors seek out fun, exciting wines at great prices, and offer them by the glass (BTG). Further outside of major metropolitan areas, you may have less of a BTG selection. This is a problem, since you may not always be in the mood to have a whole bottle for dinner. You should be aware that restaurants try very hard to make their biggest margins on wines by the glass. Sometimes buyers have a perception that people don't know or care what is being poured and those that do care will purchase bottles. Therefore, some of the selection poured BTG is a mega-brand, generic type of wine. This is very unfortunate, and I find that those establishments generally don't really understand wine and don't even bother to create a good program for their customers. Even many mega-brands have mid-tier or better selections, but often BTG offerings remain at the low-end. Restaurateurs that have no imagination, or desire to improve their wine programs believe the customer will be satisfied with anything. With all of the choices in the market today there is no excuse for this type of thinking.

As we discussed earlier, there are endless varieties of wines in the market, one better than the next. Consumers are in a position to demand better from their restaurants, so next time you are poured a dull wine by the glass, ask for something better. It is your right and for that matter responsibility to let them know they need to improve. If you don't voice your opinion, they won't know enough to do better. Not confident enough to say something? Think of it this way - do you need to be a chef to decide whether the food you were served was pleasing? It is the same with wine. Gain some control and ask more for your money. For a $7-$10 by the glass you can get a very nice glass of white wine. In that range you can also find a solid glass of red wine from Chile, Australia, Washington State, or lighter bodied wines from France such as Cotes du Rhone which are good values. Reasonably decent California Cabernets Sauvignon will be more likely in the $12-$15 range as will some Italian, Spanish, Argentinean wines. Unfortunately, while good quality Bordeaux and Burgundy reds are generally priced too high to ordinarily be served by the glass.

If you are just looking to sip and talk, stick to New World wines by the glass, which will have a bigger, fruitier mouth-feel. As you order food, Old World red wines are an excellent choice because generous acidity and earthy, savory flavors offer a way to balance the food flavors.

SUMMARY:
- For important dinners, preview the wine list. Check on line, stop by the restaurant, or have them email the wine list. It is good to be prepared.
- If you are choosing wines by the glass check if the offering is peppered with well-known brands that you see in every store. This will indicate how much effort and imagination the restaurant has put into their list.
- If it's by the glass, ASK FOR A TASTE before being poured a full glass! Restaurants allow you to taste the wines before committing to a full pour.
- Feel free to let the restaurant know if their wines by the glass were good, bad or ugly!
- While it's great to pick a glass of wine to start an evening, sometimes it's ok to wait to order bottles of wine until you and companions have decided on food selection.
- Try to give the sommelier a price range in terms of what you would like to spend.
- Let the sommelier know the type of wines you have enjoyed in the past as a guideline.
- Keep **WOW** in mind as you make selection. Rule of thumb is light foods go with lighter bodied wines, heavy dishes can take fuller bodied wines.
- Light bodied red wines also match well with fish and poultry, pork and veal. So do try dry rosé wines!
- Fruity Riesling and aromatic white wines such as Gruner Veltliner from Austria are excellent choices with Asian cuisine.

CHAPTER 7. SCREW IT

Even wine neophytes tend to voice an opinion on the question of wine closures, and this matter has been discussed in depth by people in and out of the industry, especially since we are seeing the prolific reemergence of screw-caps. Why is this a topic once again? For those who can recall, initial jug wine from California had screw cap closures back in the sixties and seventies; at that time, they dominated the American wine industry. While the industry has taken giant leaps forward, those jug wines are still on the shelves with their original screw cap closures and they are deemed to be literally bottom of the barrel in quality. So how is it that you now see hundreds of brands from all over the world losing the attachment to cork and turning to screw caps? What does it mean when you are ordering a high-end, expensive wine at a restaurant and it comes out in a screw cap bottle? Better yet, what is going on when the wine you have been buying for years turns up in a screw cap with no cork in sight? To answer that question let's consider the topic of flawed wine.

Here is a common scenario. You are hosting a dinner at a restaurant and the sommelier suggested a pricey wine, which you decided was worth the splurge. The wine is decanted and poured carefully. You try the wine and nod, all the while you are thinking there must be something wrong with your palate, because truthfully, you did not care for what you have just tasted. The wine is poured for all and everyone is nodding with appreciation. You just can't tell if they like the wine or they don't want to look foolish. The Sommelier described the wine as flavors of plum, cherry and chocolate, but all you smell are aromas of a musty wet basement. Considering you have just committed a small chunk of your wealth to this bottle, should you take a chance and send the wine back? You ask the Sommelier to come back to the table. They glare at you as you say the wine is not what you expected. They take a sip, raise an eyebrow over their black-rimmed glasses, and say the wine is "corked". The wine is replaced and now you find the flavors they described - disaster averted.

If you are in a restaurant and find yourself unhappy with how a wine tastes, don't be shy asking the Sommelier or wine buyer to taste it with you. They taste hundreds and even thousands of wines every year, and their palate will be in tune to how a wine should taste, as well as any potential flaws. It is a part of the service to help you and a sign of knowledge, as it is something confident wine professionals will do as well.

What is truly wrong with a "corked" wine? Simply put, the flaw designated as "corked" is based on a fungus, Trichloroanisole (TCA), which can occur naturally in the bark of the tree used to make the cork is occasionally present in natural cork. It has nothing to do with the quality or the price of the cork used by the winery and is a random occurrence by the time it ends up in a bottle of wine. It is widely reported that TCA can be present in 3-10% of all wines sealed with natural cork. To further complicate matters, there are degrees of the flaw. Some wines can have very faint cork taint, suppressing the aromatics and flavors of the wine, while others have an immediate and overwhelming musty, wet basement odor.

Imagine the winemaker who worked hard and succeeded in producing a fruity, well balanced wine only to have a consumer, unfortunately, open a bottle that was less than pleasing. Because the consumer never tasted this wine before, they had no idea how it should taste and that it was not normal for the wine to be dull and musty. The consumer will only know enough that they did not care for the wine, and will not purchase it again. Had they bothered to open a second bottle, they would have found a great difference. The wine would have been everything intended by the winemaker with ripe berry and cherry aromatics and flavors, however after a negative experience, that brand does not stand a second chance with this buyer.

This, then, is the greatest disservice of cork to winemakers as well as consumers, both of whom lose every time. With a screw-cap closure, this pitfall is eliminated and consumers are assured of the consistency of quality in every bottle. Often there is no price differential in producers procuring screw-caps or corks. Winemakers are not trying to stiff you by cheapening their product with screw-cap. They are simply looking to protect their wines and ensure the best possible experience for consumers. Retailers, restaurateurs, wholesalers, importers and wineries all have to deal with taking returns on bad wine, much of which is due to cork taint. Now that you have some clarity on this topic, feel confident that every screw-cap bottle will offer the best that the wine can present. You will find expensive wines such as Plumpjack Cabernet Sauvignon from Napa, as well as many New Zealand and Australian high-end wines with this closure.

You will mostly experience screw-caps in the $20 and under category of wines, mainly aromatic whites that need to be consumed within a year or two of release. We still don't have enough information on the age-ability of screw-cap wine and this is something wineries are studying right now. Because cork is porous, a minute amount of air enters the bottle over time and allows the wine to develop in a particular way. Since screw-caps seal completely, the evolution and age-ability of the wine will be different. As more data evolves, you will find wineries making a determination in terms of the type of closure for their high end bottling(s).

On occasion you might also find a glass-topped closure, which a number of European producers have already embraced. It is a glass seal that locks the wine perfectly, and allows for excellent resealing after opening. It is the most expensive solution, and makes for an elegant presentation. Much like screw-cap closures, glass does not allow for any permeation of oxygen, so age-ability there too is in question. Over time, more and more producers will embrace a variety of closures, so don't automatically assume cork is the best, or the only, quality solution especially as technology advances. Now you can feel confident in front of all wine snobs by simply pointing out the screw-cap's positive attributes and comfortable in the knowledge that the wine will mostly taste just as it should.

While there are other potential wine flaws, many of those are too complex to recognize unless you are trained professional. If you are ever sensing there could be something wrong with the taste of a wine, do ask the Sommelier to taste it with you as you are likely to be correct, and you can have that bottle replaced.

SUMMARY:
- If you think the wine is not right, ask the buyer to taste it and have him replace it for you.
- When a wine smells like a wet basement, odds are it is flawed and affected by bacteria known as TCA, commonly referred to as cork taint. It can be returned to your vendor for a full refund. Pick another bottle of the same wine and try again.
- It was NOT the wine that was bad, just the bottle.
- Up to 3-10% of all wine with cork closure can be affected by TCA.
- The worst part of cork taint is when it simply depletes the wine of all aromatics and flavors, as everything is muted. Not exactly terrible in taste, but not showing the wine's potential either.
- Price and quality of cork has no bearing cork taint. TCA does not acknowledge price points.
- Screw-cap does not mean the wine is cheap or low quality.
- Keep in mind screw-cap will guarantee that wine will be without cork-taint.
- The glass lock is the newest rage in enclosures and is the most expensive solution for the winery.

CHAPTER 8. BUBBLY

When we celebrate an event, a life milestone, the attention turns most often to Champagne as the wine of choice. Yet this category is so often misunderstood that even the word "Champagne" is at times misused. The most pervasive perspective people tend to have is that any effervescent wine is Champagne. To correct that thinking, let's first understand that Champagne, first and foremost, refers to a wine region in France. The only sparkling wine that can be referred to as Champagne **must** come from the eponymous region. Any other wine with bubbles is referred to as Sparkling Wine. This specificity for Champagne is enforced by European Union legislation, which takes into account a specific wine's place of origin.

Champagne is typically made from a blend of two red grapes and one white; Pinot Noir, Pinot Meunier and Chardonnay. There is a category called Blanc de Blanc, Champagnes with that designation are entirely made from Chardonnay. For most people it is a surprise to learn red grapes are used in Champagne, as the wines appear in the glass as white wines. The red wine color is deliberately withheld in the Champagne process because the red grapes are not allowed to macerate "on the skins". Maceration is the process wherein the grape's juice rests in contact with the grape's skins that results in deep red color for red wines. Champagne made entirely from red grapes is known as Blanc de Noir. Rose Champagne or Sparkling Wine is made from red grapes that are allowed the added period of skin contact to provide color, tannins and flavor.

There is also a known "Method Champenoise," which is the process of making Champagne in France. Other regions have adapted this wine making method to their Sparkling Wines, but that still does not permit the use of the Champagne name for their product.

The leading Champagne producers periodically make something known as "Tête de Cuvée", which is Champagne utilizing the highest quality fruit from the top vineyards in the best years.

Many winemaking regions beyond Champagne make sparkling wines, and in some cases have their own linguistic references to designate the wines. Sparkling Wine is any wine with bubbles that come from outside of the Champagne region in France. In the U.S. you can find Sparking Wines labeled as "Champagne" however there must be a region name attached to it. For example, a Sparkling Wine from California made in "Méthode Champenoise", may be labeled as "California Champagne", as long as it was using the word "Champagne" prior to 2006. With European Union treaties now in place, Champagne is reserved for Sparkling Wines produced in the Champagne region of France.

Prosecco is not a region, rather, a style of Sparkling made with a grape called Glera from Italy's Veneto region. The Italians thus far have been successful in protecting the variety name so no other region can sell wines called Prosecco. In comparison to Champagne, Prosecco tends to be lighter, fruitier and often a little sweeter. For example, the classic Italian Bellini cocktail should never be made with Champagne, as the drink requires a fruitier Sparkling Wine to complement the white peach puree. Prosecco is made in a slightly different way, called the "Transfer method", whose end result is a sparkling wine that is fruitier and lighter than wines made in "Méthode Champenoise". Prosecco wines offer value in the $9.99-$16.99 price points and are a lovely alternative to more expensive Champagne options.

Franciacorta is a designated area within Italy's Lombardy region and all sparkling wines made from there must use "Méthode Champenoise". The approved core grape varieties for production are primarily Chardonnay (white), Pinot Nero (red) and Pinot Bianco (white). Wines from this region are typically found at $35 per bottle and above in the U.S. market, creating a bit of a market challenge for the producers because they compete against the much better advertised Champagnes of France.

Cava is the Spanish Sparkling Wine, typically made from a blend of local Spanish varieties, namely the Macabeo (white), Parellada (white) and Xarel.lo (white), using "Méthode Champenoise". As described earlier, it cannot be called Champagne. Priced mostly under $20, Cava is a dry sparkling wine, not at all like the fruity Prosecco. Popular in Spain and now readily found in retail and some restaurants, Cava offers an inexpensive alternative to Champagne for day-to-day drinking.

Sekt is the German language word for Sparkling Wine, and it is produced in Germany and Austria from a variety of grapes. Those include imported grapes as well as Riesling in Germany, and Gruner Veltliner in Austria. These wines tend to be fruity and fresh, fun and affordable options for day-to-day drinking. Not much of this category can be found in the U.S. market, as Germans are avid consumers of Sparkling Wine and consume most of the domestic production. Pricing is typically under $16 per bottle.

Decisions about purchasing a bubbly should be entirely experimental. Whether Champagne or Sparkling Wine, any bottle from any country designated with "Méthode Champenoise" or "Traditionelle" will be at varying degrees of dryness as per the chart below. If it does not have this designation look for Brut, Extra Brut or similar language to indicate dryness levels. Lastly, you can count on Prosecco to be fruity, fresh, and even a little bit sweet, hence a perfect cocktail mate.

Champagne Terms	Meaning
Brut Nature/Sauvage	Extremely Dry
Brut	Dry
Extra Brut/Extra Sec	Not as Dry as Brut
Demi Sec	Half dry
Doux, Dolce	Sweet
Blanc de Blanc	Made only from Chardonnay grapes
Blanc de Noir	Made only from Pinot Noir and/or Pinot Meunier
Tete de cuvee	Flagship wine of Champagne House, best fruit from best vineyards, made in peak

SUMMARY:
- Champagne is a region of France, and it is a term that is strictly used to describe the wines made there.
- The process of making Champagne is called Méthode Champenoise.
- Typically Champagne is made in one of three styles: blend of red and white grapes, blend of only Chardonnay known as Blanc de Blanc, or only red grapes known as Blanc de Noir
- Core varieties in Champagne are Chardonnay (white), Pinot Noir (red), Pinot Meunier (red).
- "Tête de cuvée" is the top selection of a Champagne House, utilizing the best fruit from the top vineyards, and made only in the best years.
- Rose Champagne or Sparkling Wine is made from red grapes that are allowed added period of skin contact to provide color, tannins and flavor.
- Sparkling Wines are any wines with bubbles that come from any country, anywhere, outside of Champagne.
- Cava is Spanish sparkling wine that uses local grapes and Méthode Champenoise winemaking process.
- Prosecco is a Sparkling, fruity wine made from the Glara grape in the Veneto region of Italy. It is made in a slightly different way than Champagne, called the "Transfer method", whose end result is a Sparkling Wine that is lighter and softer.
- Franciacorta is an Italian Sparkling Wine from the Lombardy region, created with the Méthode Champenoise winemaking process.
- Sekt is the German word for Sparkling Wine. In Germany, the wine is made mostly from imported grapes, and at times, Riesling.
- Any Sparkling Wine from any country or region, other than Champagne, made with Méthode Champenoise will tend to be dryer than other Sparkling Wine alternatives. This does not include Prosecco

CHAPTER 9. DESSERT IN A GLASS

What exactly is dessert wine? It sounds sweet. Do you have it with dessert? In lieu of? Possibly both are correct answers? So many misconceptions, yet so many possibilities. Let's take a closer look at the oldest and greatest dessert wines of the world, as well as up-and-coming categories.

Noble Rot - Botrytis:

"Botrytized" wines are some of the most sophisticated and highly prized wines on earth, and born of a mold known as Botryitis Cynerea. Referred to as "Noble Rot", this was first discovered in Tokaj, Hungary in the early 1500's. As legend depicts, the monks were about to harvest grapes when Turkish forces attacked the region, delaying the process. Once the forces were pushed back, the monks entered the vineyard and found shriveled grapes on the vines. They went about making wine and as a result of the delayed harvest, found the wines to have an intense sweet mouthfeel. Keep in mind, there was no sugar available during the Middle Ages so anything naturally sweet was highly prized. At the same time, the natural acidity of the core grape, Furmint, balanced the sweetness with a lemony tartness.

Tokaj is not a wine or a grape, it is a region that produces many types of wines and varieties, all from white grapes. As with Champagne, the name Tokaj cannot be used by any other wine or region. The Emperor recognized the wines from this region as Tokaji with the first official wine Classification system in 1730, about 180 years before the Bordeaux Classification. Today the EU protection applies to wines from Tokaj, therefore Italy and Alsace, France and Italy have had to drop the word Tocai or Tokay from their labels. Aszu means "botrytis", so Tokaji Aszu means botrytis wine from Tokaj, Hungary.

In Tokaj grapes are picked berry-by-berry beginning in late October. It is an expensive, meticulous and long process. Once placed in stainless steel vats, the concentration of natural sugars allows the berries to seep out the sweetness in liquid form. It is this liquid that is added to a base wine and the winemaker, according to the laws of the region, determines the sweetness concentration level of the final product. It is indicated on the bottles as 3, 4, 5 or 6 Puttonyos, in ascending order of sweetness. The most prized wine in this category is the Tokaji Eszencia, which is simply the pure, uncut botrytized juice from the grape. It is mostly available at auction houses, can costs thousands of dollars per bottle and has only 1%-2% alcohol. Tokaji Aszu and Eszencia can reportedly age for hundreds of years.

Sauternes is part of the Graves region of Bordeaux, France where they produce the renowned dessert wine. The core white grape varieties of white Bordeaux wine is Semillion, Sauvignon Blanc, and Muscadelle. These are the grapes at the core of Sauternes wines. In order to make the sweet wines, harvest is delayed to allow the grapes to be infected by Noble Rot, "Botrytis". As in Tokaji, the mold dries out the grapes, shrinking them into raisin-like fruit with a high concentration of natural sugars. One of the oldest and most famous producers is Chateau d'Yquem.

Known for its lovely Rieslings, Germany is also a hotbed of tremendous dessert wines in a several categories: Beerenauslese (BA), Trockenbeerenauslese (TBA) and Eiswein. Beerenauslese has nice concentration of natural sugars, but also high acidity when compared to TBA. This occurs because the berries are only partially infected with Noble Rot. TBA's are fully based on Botrytis berries so are markedly richer in mouthfeel and denser in natural sugar levels. German winemakers also produce a fair amount of Eiswein (Ice Wine), which is a different harvest process from Beerenauslese and TBA's. Ice wine is made by winemakers leaving grapes on the vine through December. As the grapes encounter freezing temperatures, they are harvested during the night. These berries are not infected by Botrytis, so they typically can have higher acidity. All of these wines are made from the Riesling grape, as that is the core German variety.

Ice Wine:

In the last decade Canada has become known for its Ice Wine category and interestingly enough, their Ice Wines are made from both red and white grapes. Since the climate is cold many varieties would not survive, but cool climate grapes such as Riesling, Cabernet Franc and Pinot Noir can do well in Canadian winemaking regions. Ice Wines are produced from all three of the grapes and are highly prized. Ice Wine is made in other regions of the world, but very often from lab-frozen grapes, while both German and Canadian production works with naturally frozen grapes.

Fortified Wines:

When hard alcohol/spirit is added to a base wine, this is called fortification. Historically, alcohol was added to base wines to prevent spoilage or spontaneous re-fermentation while on long journeys to far away overseas markets such as England. However, this resulted in high levels of alcohol. The most famous fortified wine is Port, which comes from the Duoro region of Portugal. Most Port is made from red grapes, but some white Port wines are available as well. There are three types of Port to consider; Ruby Port, which is sweet, easy going, red in color, and an early drinking wine aged only three years. It is also the most affordable in terms of price. Tawny Port is golden brown in color, and is designated as a 10, 20, 30 or 40-year-old as in the average aged wines that were blended to create the wine. The most expensive type is Vintage Port, which is only made in the best of years. These wines pair beautifully with any type of chocolate dessert, and also a whole range of cheeses.

Sherry originated in Southern Spain, where brandy was added to base wine to produce an intensely alcoholic liquid, which could result in a sweet or dry expression. Sherry is made from several vintages of wines. Madeira is also a fortified wine made from four grapes, and comes from an island off the coast of Portugal.

SUMMARY:
- There are several types of dessert wines, both fortified and naturally sweet.
- Under certain climactic conditions, Botrytis is a natural fungus that infects grapes as they shrivel. Botrytis is key to very intense levels of sugar concentration in a grape.
- As Botrytis grapes are added to base wine, a natural sweetness develops. Most notably this process was developed in Tokaj, Hungary in the Middle Ages.
- The core grape variety for this process is Furmint.
- Tokaj is a wine region, not a grape.
- Other famous regions producing Botrytis based naturally sweet wines include Sauternes in Bordeaux France, where the dessert wine is made from Sauvignon Blanc and Semillion.
- Wine regions throughout Germany also produce Botrytis based dessert wines from the Riesling grape.
- Late harvest dessert wines have less intense sweetness and are made throughout the world. Late harvest means late picked grapes are harvested, as the longer you leave grapes on the vine, the natural sugar levels rise.
- For Botrytis dessert wines the best matches include any type of fruit based desserts or blue cheeses.
- Canada and Germany are famous for naturally made Ice Wines, which are made when frost hits the vineyards. Ice wine can also be made with frozen grapes, once sugar levels reach the desired sweetness.
- Fortified wines are made from a base wine to which alcohol (mostly brandy) is added.
- Examples of fortified wines are Port, Sherry, Madeira.
- Port comes from the Duoro region of Portugal, and comes in three core styles: Easy drinking Ruby Port, Tawny Port and the ultra premium category of Vintage Port.
- Sherry is a fortified wine that comes from Spain, but can be dry or sweet.
- Madeira comes from an island in Portugal, and is a fortified wine made from four grape varieties.
- Best Pairing for Port is anything chocolate, all types of blue cheese and walnuts.

Chapter 10. PINK IS IN – A ROSE BY ANY NAME

The dry rose wine craze has caught many by surprise, but the style of wine has been around for ages. In Europe these wines have been a tradition of the summer set in many vacation resorts, from South of France to lake and ocean resorts. U.S. consumers have been late to the trend, however rose sales have been rising astronomically in recent years. What's not to love? It's pink, with red berry flavors, delicious, and pairs well with light dishes.

The American wine consumer dabbling with White Zinfandel of the 1980's and 90's is mostly gone, as those wines had nothing to do with dry rose as we associate it with France. White Zin was mostly very sweet and cheap, and had a following from entry level wine consumers. Lovers of the dry rose styles have been enthralled with the pale pink hues of roses mostly from Provence, France. Provence as a wine region has captured the imagination of critics and wine lovers alike, yielding pink magic in bottle after bottle. Now with some added celebrity fanfare, dry roses are here to stay, and are not just for summer any more.

As much as you would still drink a white wine any time of the year, rose is a wine to have in the mix as it is eminently quaffable, On a **WOW** scale it is mostly rated in the **(1)** category pairing well with seafood, white meats, and vegetarian dishes. While Provence has been leading the charge, other parts of France and the world are making lovely roses worth trying.

While it is not so much a factor for enjoyment, it is good to have an idea about how rose wines are made. Rose wines are made with red grapes in primarily one of two ways. One way is the "direct press", where red grape clusters are harvested and pressed after a very brief contact between the juice and grape skins, leading to a pale pink hue. This is a method used by most Provence winemakers.

In the "Soignee" method, the goal is to make intense red wine, and some of the juice is run off during a more extended maceration in order to concentrate the flavors in the remaining red wine. The run off juice is then turned into a rose, but in this case, it is viewed as a byproduct of the red wine. This method typically delivers a deeper pink color, with more of a full bodied wine. In this case, Soignee method roses tend to be a **(2)** on the **WOW** scale.

While both methods work well, clearly the wine selection is more of a personal choice. A bright, delicate, acidic, zippy rose tends to be from the direct press approach and fuller bodied experience can be had from the Soignee method. You can guess by looking at the color, however neither process is an assurance of quality. The quality is determined by the winery and the winemaker, so if you find a brand you enjoy, take note. With thousands of producers and brands making pink juice in a range of quality levels and styles, one would consider price as a great indicator. However, with rose, this is not necessarily the case. It is still possible to have a delicious rose at $12.99 or less, so don't be too sure that buying that high flying, expensive brand of the moment will give you a greater experience in the glass.

Provence rose tend to be made from a blend of any of the following grapes: Grenache, Syrah, Cinsault, Carignan, Tibouren and Mouvedre grapes, while California roses gravitate towards Cabernet, Merlot or Pinot Noir. In Italy Sangiovese is often used, while Spanish rosados come from Tempranillo. Essentially all growing regions focus on their core red grapes for rose wines. Regardless of grape and color, these are fun expressions of the rose category, and well worth some experimentation.

SUMMARY:
- Dry rose wine is not White Zinfandel.
- Dry rose is made one of two ways; Direct Press or Soignee.
- In Direct Press the red grape clusters are harvested and pressed after a very brief contact between the juice and grape skins, leading to a pale pink hue.
- In Direct Press method the goal is to make a great rose wine.
- Direct Press is a method used by most Provence (France) winemakers.
- In the Soignee method, the goal is to make an intense red wine.
- Using the Soignee method, some of the juice is run off during a more extended maceration in order to concentrate the flavors in the remaining red wine.
- The run off pale juice can be turned into a rose wine.
- Soignee typically delivers a deeper pink color, with more of a full bodied wine.
- In this case, Direct Press roses tend to be a **WOW (1)** while Soignee method roses tend to be a **(2)** on the **WOW** scale.
- Provence is a leader in the dry rose movement, but lovely dry roses are made in other French regions as well as the rest of the world.
- Provence rose tend to be made from a blend of any of the following grapes: Grenache, Syrah, Cinsault, Carignan, Tibouren and Mouvedre grapes.
- California roses gravitate towards Cabernet, Merlot or Pinot Noir. In Italy Sangiovese is often used, while Spanish rosados come from Tempranillo.
- The other regions typically use the Soignee method and produce fuller bodied rose wines.
- All growing regions focus on their core red grapes for rose wines

CHAPTER 11. HOW TO LOOK GOOD DRINKING WINE

Start at home. If you have the old style, small wine glasses, it is time for a change. I am not advocating expensive glassware, but do look for nice big bowls so you can better practice swirling and thereby ultimately  improve the flavor of any wine. Two standard type of glasses apply. The straight-lipped bowl is meant for Bordeaux type wines including all three grape types that we just covered in the Bordeaux chapter, whereas the very round bowl is for both white and red Burgundy varieties. Slightly smaller straight lipped glassware is perfect for ubiquitous whites and even dessert wines. If you are unsure about what to use, just save the very round bowls for Chardonnay and Pinot Noir and use the Bordeaux glasses for everything else.

As practice for a proper swirl, take a wine glass and fill it with about two ounces of water. Place the wine glass on a table or countertop, and secure the foot of the stem between your index and third fingers. The focus here is on swirling wine without spilling, and agitating. This is how the pros do it.

Here you are with water in the glass, glass stem between your fingers, making small, tight, counter clock-wise circles about two inches in diameter, letting the liquid swirl in your glass. This is the first thing that separates people who actually know wine from those who don't. I can't tell you how many "collectors" with great wine cellars don't know how to do this properly. All wine professionals start with the swirl. It allows the wine aromas to open up by infusing oxygen, and suddenly the flavors become more pronounced. Take five to ten seconds or more. As you progress with swirling skills, you will do this motion in the air. Caution. Do not try this yet. Stick to what works, and look good doing it. If you have mastered this with water, try it with wine - white at first. And it doesn't hurt to wear black, just in case!

Next mistake wine lovers make is that while enjoying wine, they grasp the wine glass by the bowl. PLEASE DON'T DO THIS, unless the wine is very cold. Touching the bowl changes the temperature, so hold a wine glass by the stem. It allows the temperature of the wine to stay at the appropriate serving temperature, and this is the accepted wine-pro "look".

By now we have swirled, and it is time to smell the wine. Breathe in the wine aromas for a full second or two, but no more. Observe the color. After that, take a sip, and let it move around your mouth. Then swallow.

When attending a wine tasting event, don't fall into the trap of familiarity. TASTE EVERYTHING! Smell, swirl, sip and spit. That is how wine pros are able to taste numerous wines without falling over. Do not gravitate to the wines and varieties you usually enjoy. Have a small sip instead of numerous wines to build a palate library of flavors. It is best to do all white wines first, followed by rose, and then red wines. Save dessert for last. This way the **WOW** will keep your palate relatively fresh, as tasting a big red wine would kill your taste buds for anything subtler, and it would be hard to recover in time to taste a light, aromatic white wine.

SUMMARY:
- At wine events, TASTE EVERYTHING. Smell, swirl, sip and spit.
- Round bowls are for Pinot Noir and Chardonnay, and are referred to as "Burgundy" glasses.
- Straight lipped stemware is referred to as "Bordeaux" glassware, meant originally for the Bordeaux varieties, and can be used for all other non-Burgundy grapes.
- To taste a wine, choose the appropriate wine glass, and pour about two-finger widths of wine, which is enough so you can swirl comfortably without spilling.
- Always hold wine glasses by the stem. Holding the bowl of a wine glass will change temperature of the wine.
- Swirl like a pro by having a glass on the table, then placing the foot of the stem between your index and third fingers and making counter clock-wise tight circles to open up the wine's aromatics and flavors.
- If you are feeling very confident, try the same motion in the air, with only your wrists making small circles. Try it using water first!
- Swirl, smell, observe the color, then sip and let the wine move around in your mouth, finally swallow.
- At wine tastings focus on white wines first, followed by rose, red wines and lastly dessert wines. It will allow you to taste like a professional, keeping in mind the **WOW** principles we just covered.
- The whole point of wine tasting is the experimentation; try a sip of many wines you would never order. It is the best way to expand your enjoyment and knowledge.

Voila! Relax, swirl, smell, sip and enjoy!

Monika Elling is the CEO and Founder of Foundations Marketing Group, a brand development agency launched in 2010 to address the growing strategic needs of the wine, spirits and luxury product sectors. She is also Founder of The Paradigm Collection, a fine wine and craft spirits importer.

Monika has years of trade, in supply, import and distribution, having previously served as Director of Public Relations at Lauber Imports, a division of Southern Wines & Spirits, America's largest wholesaler. She is a thought leader and innovator in the global wine and spirits industry, and created a unique platform to embrace the latest market innovations.

Monika is a noted speaker and author, and a regular presenter at numerous industry events, such as the Society of Wine Educators Conferences.

Made in the USA
Columbia, SC
31 October 2017